# Routines for Success

# Routines for Success

## Daily Habits to Boost Productivity and Achieve Your Goals

Maykel Bustamante C

Copyright © 2024 Maykel Bustamante Corrales
All rights reserved.

Dedication:

To everyone facing difficult times, this book is for you.

Life's challenges may seem overwhelming at times, but remember that each new day brings with it the opportunity to rebuild, grow, and find strength you never knew you had. May these routines serve as small steps towards regaining control, hope, and a renewed sense of purpose. Keep going, even when the path seems uncertain. You are stronger than you think, and brighter days are ahead.

# Summary

Introduction: A Step-by-Step Guide to Building Routines That Lead to Success --------7

Chapter 1: Morning Routines for Success --------10

Chapter 2: Building a Productive Work Routine --------14

Chapter 3: Incorporating Healthy Habits into Your Day --------20

Chapter 4: Routines to Boost Mental Clarity and Focus --------29

Chapter 5: Routines for Personal Growth and Learning --------37

Chapter 6: Evening Routines for Reflection and Relaxation --------44

Chapter 7: Routines to Build Strong Relationships --------54

Chapter 8: Customizing and Evolving Your Routines --------64

Conclusion --------73

Bibliography --------76

# Introduction: A Step-by-Step Guide to Building Routines That Lead to Success

Success is often seen as a result of talent, hard work, or even luck. While these elements play a part, there's one factor that often goes unnoticed: routines. What we do every day—our habits and rituals—ultimately shape our lives and lead us towards either success or stagnation.

Think of highly successful individuals, whether they are entrepreneurs, athletes, or creatives. Behind every accomplishment lies a foundation of daily routines that help them stay focused, energized, and disciplined. These routines aren't random; they are carefully designed systems meant to maximize productivity, enhance well-being, and ensure consistent progress towards their goals.

In this book, we will explore the power of daily routines and how you can create your own success system. From the moment you wake up to the time you go to sleep, your day can be filled with intentional actions that propel you towards a better version of yourself. We'll break down the essential components of effective routines and provide you with practical tips on how to incorporate them into your life.

## Why Routines Matter

Routines provide structure in a world full of distractions. When you have a clear plan for your day, you reduce decision fatigue and free up mental energy for more important tasks. Routines also build discipline and consistency, two key ingredients for long-term success. By automating certain actions—like waking up early, exercising, or setting goals—you eliminate the guesswork and make it easier to stay on track.

## What to Expect

Throughout this book, you'll learn how to:

- Design a powerful morning routine that sets a productive tone for your day.
- Build a work routine that keeps you focused and efficient.
- Incorporate healthy habits to support your physical and mental well-being.
- Develop a night routine that helps you unwind and prepare for the next day.

Each chapter will guide you step-by-step through the process of building these routines, complete with actionable advice, examples, and exercises. By the end of this book, you will have a personalized routine designed to optimize your daily performance and accelerate your path to success.

# Chapter 1: Morning Routines for Success

The way you start your morning can set the tone for the rest of your day. Successful people often attribute their productivity and focus to the routines they follow every morning. A well-structured morning routine helps you take control of your day, reduce stress, and prepare both mentally and physically for the challenges ahead.

In this chapter, we'll explore the key elements of a powerful morning routine that will boost your energy, sharpen your focus, and position you for success.

## Wake Up Early

One of the most common traits of successful individuals is their ability to wake up early. The early hours of the day are quiet, free from distractions, and provide an opportunity for uninterrupted time to focus on yourself.

- **Benefits:** More time to plan your day, mental clarity, and a sense of accomplishment from the start.
- **How to Implement It:** Begin by setting a consistent sleep schedule, aiming for 7-8 hours of rest. Avoid using screens (phones, laptops) at least 30 minutes before bed to help you unwind. Use a gradual alarm that wakes you up gently rather than a jarring noise that can trigger stress from the moment you open your eyes.

## Practice Mindfulness or Meditation

Starting your day with mindfulness or meditation helps your thoughts and prepare for whatever lies ahead. It fosters calmness, reduces anxiety, and allows you to focus on your priorities with a clear mind.

- **Mindfulness Exercise:** Spend 5-10 minutes in silence, focusing on your breathing. Allow any thoughts to pass without judgment and gently return your focus to your breath.
- **Gratitude or Reflection:** Alternatively, you can spend this time writing down three things you're grateful for or reflecting on your intentions for the day. This practice can shift your mindset towards positivity and purpose.

## Engage in Physical Activity

Physical exercise is essential for boosting both energy and mental clarity. You don't need a long workout to see benefits; even 10-15 minutes of movement in the morning can make a significant difference.

- **Simple Exercises:** Yoga, stretching, or a quick walk can do wonders to wake up your body. If you prefer a more intense routine, bodyweight exercises like push-ups, squats, or jumping jacks are effective.

- **Benefits:** Exercise releases endorphins, which improve mood, reduce stress, and sharpen your focus for the tasks ahead.

## Plan Your Day

Taking a few minutes each morning to organize your day is one of the most powerful habits you can develop. Planning reduces decision fatigue, keeps you focused, and helps you stay productive.

- **Prioritize:** Identify the three most important tasks (MITs) you need to accomplish that day. These should be your primary focus.
- **Time Management:** Use techniques like time blocking or the Pomodoro method to structure your day effectively. Allocate time for your MITs and ensure you schedule breaks to recharge.
- **Review Your Calendar:** Check your appointments, deadlines, and meetings to ensure you're prepared.

## Fuel Your Body with a Healthy Breakfast

What you eat in the morning plays a crucial role in your energy levels and cognitive function throughout the day. A balanced breakfast helps stabilize blood sugar, improve concentration, and maintain energy.

- **Healthy Choices:** Foods that provide sustained energy, like oatmeal, eggs, fruit, or smoothies packed with greens and protein.

- **Avoid:** Sugary cereals or refined carbohydrates, which can lead to energy crashes later in the day.

# Chapter 2: Building a Productive Work Routine

In today's fast-paced world, distractions are everywhere—emails, social media, phone notifications, and endless meetings. Without a clear work routine, it's easy to lose focus, waste time, and feel overwhelmed. However, a well-structured work routine can help you maximize your productivity, keep you on track with your goals, and create a sustainable balance between work and personal life.

In this chapter, we'll explore how to design a productive work routine that minimizes distractions, optimizes your time, and ensures you make meaningful progress every day.

## Prioritize Your Tasks

One of the most critical aspects of a productive work routine is learning how to prioritize. Not all tasks are created equal—some will have a greater impact on your progress than others. By identifying and focusing on your most important tasks (MITs), you'll make the most out of your workday.

- **Identify Your MITs:** Start by making a list of all the tasks you need to accomplish. Then, ask yourself which ones will have the biggest impact on your goals. These should be your top priorities. Ideally, aim for 2-3 MITs per day.

- **Eat the Frog:** A popular concept from Brian Tracy, "Eat the Frog" suggests that you tackle your hardest or most dreaded task first thing in the morning. Once it's out of the way, the rest of your day will feel easier, and you'll avoid procrastination.

## Time Blocking for Maximum Efficiency

Time blocking is a powerful technique for managing your time effectively. Instead of working randomly throughout the day, you schedule specific blocks of time for different tasks or types of work. This helps you stay focused and avoid multitasking, which can significantly reduce your productivity.

- **How to Time Block:** At the start of your workday, look at your tasks and allocate time slots for each. For example, you might dedicate 9-10 a.m. to email management, 10:30-12 p.m. to project work, and 2-3 p.m. for meetings.

- **The 90-Minute Rule:** Research shows that our brains work best in cycles of 90 minutes of focused work, followed by a short break. Try breaking your day into 90-minute blocks for high-focus tasks, followed by a 10–15-minute rest.

- **Avoid Overloading:** Be realistic with your time blocks and ensure you allow room for unexpected interruptions or delays. It's better to under-schedule and finish early than to overload yourself and feel overwhelmed.

## Minimize Distractions

Distractions are the biggest enemies of productivity. Whether it's a phone buzzing with notifications, co-workers stopping by, or social media tempting you, it's essential to create an environment that minimizes distractions.

- **Turn Off Notifications:** Set your phone to "Do Not Disturb" mode or, better yet, put it in another room during focused work time. Mute non-essential notifications on your computer, such as emails and social media.

- **Create a Dedicated Workspace:** Whether you're working from home or in an office, having a designated space for work helps train your brain to associate that area with focus. Make sure it's organized and free from distractions.

- **Batch Process Distractions:** Set specific times to check emails, messages, or social media, instead of reacting to them throughout the day. You might allocate two 30-minute slots, one in the morning and one in the afternoon, for communication tasks.

## Embrace the Pomodoro Technique

The Pomodoro Technique is a time management method designed to help you maintain focus and productivity throughout the day. It involves working in short, focused intervals (usually 25 minutes), followed by a 5-minute break.

- How It Works:
    1. Choose a task you want to work on.
    2. Set a timer for 25 minutes and work on the task without interruptions.
    3. After 25 minutes, take a 5-minute break to stretch, walk around, or relax.

4. Repeat this cycle four times, then take a longer break (15-30 minutes).

- **Why It Works:** The Pomodoro Technique prevents burnout by balancing focus with regular rest. It also helps you build a sense of urgency, as the timer encourages you to stay focused on the task at hand.

## Managing Meetings Efficiently

Meetings are often necessary, but they can also be time-consuming and inefficient if not managed properly. To maintain productivity, it's important to ensure that your meetings are purposeful and concise.

- **Set Clear Agendas:** Always have a clear agenda for each meeting. This ensures that everyone knows the purpose of the meeting and helps keep discussions focused and on track.
- **Time Limit Your Meetings:** Set strict time limits for meetings, such as 30 or 60 minutes. Encourage participants to stick to the agenda and avoid going off-topic.
- **Decline Unnecessary Meetings:** If a meeting doesn't require your input or could be resolved with an email, don't be afraid to decline or suggest alternatives.

## Take Regular Breaks

It may seem counterintuitive, but taking regular breaks can significantly enhance your productivity. Our brains have a limited capacity for focus, and working without breaks can lead to burnout, fatigue, and decreased performance.

- **The Power of Microbreaks:** A microbreak is a short, 1–2-minute break that allows you to step away from your work and refresh your mind. You can stretch, take a few deep breaths, or look away from your screen to reduce eye strain.

- **Movement Breaks:** Every hour, try to stand up and move around for at least 5 minutes. Walking or light stretching can increase circulation and improve your focus when you return to work.

## End Your Workday with a Wrap-Up Routine

Just as a strong morning routine sets the tone for your day, a productive workday should end with a wrap-up routine. This helps you reflect on what you've accomplished and prepares you for the next day.

- **Review Your Day:** Take 5-10 minutes at the end of your workday to review what you've accomplished. Did you complete your MITs? Were there any distractions or obstacles that slowed your progress?

- **Plan for Tomorrow:** Set your top priorities for the next day. This helps you hit the ground running in the morning and reduces decision fatigue.

- **Log Off:** When your workday is done, it's important to mentally and physically disconnect from work. Close your computer, tidy up your workspace, and give yourself permission to shift into relaxation mode.

A productive work routine is about more than just getting tasks done. It's about creating a system that minimizes distractions, maximizes your focus, and ensures that you're working efficiently towards your goals. By prioritizing tasks, embracing time management techniques like time blocking and the Pomodoro method, and taking regular breaks, you'll find yourself accomplishing more in less time. Additionally, by mastering the art of managing meetings and ending your day with intention, you'll create a balanced, sustainable routine that drives long-term success.

# Chapter 3: Incorporating Healthy Habits into Your Day

Success is not just about being productive or achieving your goals; it's about sustaining your energy, well-being, and mental clarity over the long term. Healthy habits are the foundation of this sustainability. They not only fuel your body but also nurture your mind, enabling you to face challenges with resilience and a positive outlook.

Incorporating health-focused habits into your routine can seem daunting at first, but small, consistent actions make a big difference. In this chapter, we'll explore how to integrate habits that boost your physical and mental health into your daily routine, providing you with the energy and focus needed to reach your goals while maintaining balance.

## The Importance of Physical Exercise

Regular physical activity is essential for maintaining your energy levels, keeping your body healthy, and improving your mental clarity. While it might seem difficult to squeeze in exercise during a busy day, even small amounts of daily movement can transform your productivity and overall well-being.

- Physical and Mental Benefits of Exercise:
    - Increased energy levels: Exercise enhances blood circulation, delivering oxygen and nutrients to your

tissues. This means more energy to power through your day.
- Improved cognitive function: Physical activity stimulates the brain and encourages the release of endorphins, which boost mood and mental focus.
- Stress reduction: Exercise triggers the production of endorphins, the body's natural mood enhancers, helping to alleviate stress, anxiety, and depression.
- Better sleep quality: People who engage in regular physical activity tend to fall asleep faster and enjoy deeper sleep cycles, which improves overall mental and physical recovery.

- How to Integrate Exercise into Your Daily Routine:
    - Start small: Don't feel pressured to begin with intense workouts. Start with activities you enjoy, like walking, stretching, or yoga, and gradually build up your routine.
    - Exercise at home: You don't need a gym to work out. You can perform bodyweight exercises like squats, push-ups, or planks right in your living room. Fitness apps and online classes can also guide you through effective workouts.
    - Take movement breaks: Incorporate movement throughout your day by taking short, active breaks. For example, stand up and stretch every hour or take a 5-minute walk around your home or office.
    - Consistency is key: Rather than focusing on intensity, aim to make exercise a consistent part of your day. Schedule it like any other important task, whether it's a quick morning run, an afternoon walks, or an evening yoga session.

# Prioritizing Nutrition for Sustained Energy

Your body is like a machine—it needs the right fuel to function optimally. Eating a balanced diet is essential for maintaining steady energy levels throughout the day and supporting both physical and mental performance. What you eat can directly impact your focus, mood, and productivity.

- **Building Balanced Meals:**
    - **Protein:** Essential for muscle repair, hormone production, and maintaining satiety. Include lean sources like chicken, fish, tofu, or legumes in your meals.
    - **Healthy fats:** Fats like avocados, nuts, seeds, and olive oil are important for brain function and keeping you full longer.
    - **Complex carbohydrates:** Whole grains, sweet potatoes, and quinoa provide long-lasting energy and stabilize blood sugar levels, helping you avoid energy crashes.
    - **Fruits and vegetables:** These provide vitamins, minerals, and antioxidants, which help protect your body from illness and improve overall health.
- **Healthy Snacking:**
    - **Avoid energy spikes and crashes:** Processed snacks like sugary cereals, cookies, or chips cause your blood sugar levels to spike, followed by an inevitable crash. Instead, choose snacks that provide a balance of nutrients, such as mixed nuts, Greek yogurt, or fresh fruits.
    - **Snack preparation:** Make healthy choices more accessible by preparing snacks in advance. Keep ready-

to-eat fruits, veggie sticks, or a handful of nuts at your desk or in your bag.

- **Hydration:**
    - **Drink water regularly:** Staying hydrated is key to maintaining energy, focus, and overall well-being. Dehydration can lead to fatigue, headaches, and difficulty concentrating.
    - **Tip:** Carry a reusable water bottle with you as a reminder to drink throughout the day. Adding slices of fruit or herbs like mint can make it more appealing.

# The Power of Sleep

Sleep is often undervalued in a world that glorifies "hustling" and working long hours. However, adequate sleep is crucial for cognitive function, memory consolidation, emotional regulation, and physical recovery. Lack of sleep affects every aspect of your life—from your mood to your ability to make decisions and solve problems effectively.

- **How Much Sleep Do You Need?**
    - **Optimal sleep range:** Most adults need between 7 and 8 hours of sleep per night for optimal functioning. Sleep deprivation, even if minimal, can impair cognitive abilities and lower productivity.
    - **Identify your sleep patterns:** Experiment with your sleep schedule to find the right amount of sleep that leaves you feeling refreshed and energized.
- **Creating a Sleep Routine:**

- **Wind down gradually:** Start winding down at least 30-60 minutes before bedtime. Avoid stimulating activities such as checking emails or engaging in emotionally charged conversations.
- **Screen-free zone:** Limit exposure to screens (phone, TV, computers) before bed, as the blue light emitted can interfere with melatonin production and disrupt your sleep cycle.
- **Relaxation techniques:** Consider incorporating relaxing activities like reading, stretching, or listening to calming music before bed to signal your body that it's time to rest.

- **Napping for Energy:**
  - **Short naps:** If you find yourself feeling fatigued during the day, consider taking a power nap. A 20–30-minute nap can restore energy and improve alertness without leaving you groggy.
  - **Avoid late naps:** To maintain a regular sleep schedule, avoid napping too late in the day, as it can interfere with nighttime sleep

## Managing Stress Through Mindfulness and Relaxation

Stress is an unavoidable part of life, but how you manage it can make all the difference. Chronic stress can take a toll on both your physical and mental health, affecting your ability to stay focused and productive. Incorporating stress-relieving practices into your daily routine can improve your resilience and overall well-being.

- **Mindfulness Practices:**

- **Mindful breathing:** One of the simplest ways to manage stress is by practicing deep breathing exercises. Take 5 minutes to close your eyes, breathe slowly, and focus on each inhale and exhale. This helps calm your mind and reduce anxiety.

- **Meditation:** Regular meditation—even for just 10 minutes a day—can reduce stress, improve focus, and enhance emotional well-being. You can use guided meditation apps or simply sit in silence, observing your thoughts without judgment.

- **Gratitude journaling:** Writing down what you're grateful for each day can help shift your focus away from stressors and toward positive aspects of your life.

- **Physical Relaxation:**

    - **Progressive muscle relaxation:** Tense and then release each muscle group in your body, starting from your toes and working your way up. This can help relieve physical tension and bring awareness to areas of stress.

    - **Stretching:** Incorporate gentle stretches into your day to release built-up tension, especially if you spend long hours sitting at a desk.

## Building Healthy Tech Habits

Technology is a powerful tool, but excessive screen time can have negative effects on your health. From eye strain to sleep disruption and increased stress, being constantly connected can take a toll on your well-being. Developing healthy tech habits allows you to harness technology without it interfering with your productivity or health.

- **Set Boundaries with Technology:**

- **Establish tech-free times:** Create designated times during the day when you step away from technology. This could be during meals, before bed, or while spending time with family and friends.

- **Use the "Do Not Disturb" mode:** During focused work or relaxation periods, turn on "Do Not Disturb" on your devices to limit distractions.

- **Taking Care of Your Eyes:**

  - **The 20-20-20 Rule:** Every 20 minutes, take a 20-second break to look at something 20 feet away. This reduces eye strain from prolonged screen time.

  - **Adjust screen brightness:** Use apps or adjust your device's settings to reduce blue light in the evening, or consider wearing blue light-blocking glasses.

- **Tech-Free Morning and Evening Routines:**

  - **Start and end your day without screens:** Avoid reaching for your phone first thing in the morning or before bed. Instead, use this time for journaling, stretching, or meditation to set a positive tone for your day and improve your sleep quality.

Incorporating healthy habits into your daily routine is essential for maintaining your physical, mental, and emotional well-being. By integrating regular exercise, nutritious meals, proper sleep, mindfulness practices, and healthy technology use, you can create a strong foundation that supports your success. These small but consistent actions will help you sustain the energy, focus, and clarity you need to achieve your long-term goals while enjoying a balanced and fulfilling life.

# Chapter 4: Routines to Boost Mental Clarity and Focus

In today's world, we are constantly bombarded with distractions—notifications, emails, social media, and an ever-growing list of tasks. With so much vying for our attention, staying focused can feel like an uphill battle. Mental clarity and focus are essential not only for productivity but also for making better decisions and staying calm in the face of challenges.

Establishing daily routines that enhance mental clarity and sharpen your focus will empower you to approach your tasks with precision and confidence. In this chapter, we will explore practical techniques and habits that you can implement to declutter your mind, reduce distractions, and maintain focus throughout your day.

## The Power of Mindfulness and Meditation for Focus

Mindfulness and meditation are powerful tools for improving mental clarity. By training your mind to stay present, you can prevent mental fog, reduce stress, and regain control over your thoughts. These practices help you sharpen your focus, making it easier to concentrate on what truly matters.

- **What is Mindfulness?**
    - **Definition:** Mindfulness is the practice of staying fully present in the moment, aware of your thoughts,

feelings, and environment without judgment. It's about observing rather than reacting.

- **Why it matters:** By practicing mindfulness, you become more aware of distractions and are better equipped to let them pass without getting caught up in them.

- **Meditation for Mental Clarity:**

    - **Starting small:** You don't need to meditate for hours to see benefits. Start with just 5-10 minutes each morning or during a break.

    - **Guided vs. unguided:** If you're new to meditation, you might find it helpful to use guided meditation apps or videos, which lead you through the process. Alternatively, you can meditate on your own by focusing on your breath or a calming phrase.

    - **Breathing exercises:** Focusing on your breath can help clear mental fog. Practice deep breathing—inhale for a count of four, hold for four, exhale for four, and repeat.

- **Mindful Practices Throughout the Day:**

    - **Single-tasking:** Instead of multitasking, practice giving your full attention to one task at a time. Mindful single-tasking not only increases focus but also improves the quality of your work.

    - **Mindful breaks:** Take a few moments during the day to practice mindfulness. Whether it's a short breathing exercise, a stretch, or simply stepping outside to observe your surroundings, these mindful breaks can reset your focus.

# Decluttering Your Mind

Mental clutter, like unresolved tasks, worries, or excessive information, can weigh you down and make it difficult to focus. Taking steps to declutter your mind will create space for more clarity, better decision-making, and a more relaxed state of being.

- **The "Brain Dump" Technique:**
    - **What it is:** A brain dump involves writing down every thought, task, and worry that's cluttering your mind. It's a way to get everything out on paper, so you don't have to carry it around in your head.
    - **How to do it:** Set aside 10-15 minutes at the beginning or end of your day to write down everything that's on your mind—tasks, ideas, worries, and random thoughts. This clears mental space and allows you to prioritize what's truly important.

- **Organize and Prioritize:**
    - **To-do lists:** Once you've written down everything, categorize your tasks. Prioritize the ones that need immediate attention and delegate or postpone tasks that aren't urgent. This prevents overwhelm and helps you focus on what matters most.
    - **The Eisenhower Matrix:** This is a simple tool for prioritizing tasks based on their urgency and importance. It divides tasks into four categories: important and urgent, important but not urgent, urgent but not important, and neither urgent nor important. Focus your energy on the tasks that are important and urgent.

- **Minimalism for Mental Clarity:**
    - **Simplify your environment:** Physical clutter can contribute to mental clutter. Clear your workspace and living areas to create a more serene environment. A

minimalist space can reduce distractions and make it easier to focus.

- o **Digital declutter:** Organize your digital life by clearing out unnecessary files, emails, and apps. A cluttered digital space can slow down your productivity and cause mental strain. Schedule regular times to clean up your inbox and desktop.

## The Role of Breaks in Enhancing Focus

Contrary to popular belief, working non-stop is not the key to productivity. Our brains need regular breaks to maintain focus and avoid burnout. Taking intentional breaks throughout the day can help reset your attention and boost mental clarity.

- **Types of Breaks:**
    - o **Active breaks:** Engage in physical movement during your break, such as stretching, walking, or light exercise. This boosts circulation, relieves tension, and helps recharge your brain.
    - o **Mental rest:** Give your mind a chance to relax by engaging in a low-effort activity like reading, doodling, or simply staring out the window.
    - o **Social breaks:** Spend a few minutes chatting with a friend or colleague. Social interaction can improve mood and mental sharpness.

## Limiting Distractions

Distractions are everywhere, and they're one of the biggest threats to focus and productivity. However, by implementing a few key strategies, you can create an environment that minimizes interruptions and allows you to concentrate on the task at hand.

- **Create a Distraction-Free Environment:**
    - **Dedicated workspace:** Designate a specific space for work or focus activities. Make sure it's free from clutter and distractions like noisy environments or unnecessary gadgets.
    - **Noise management:** If you're easily distracted by sounds, consider using noise-canceling headphones or listening to white noise or instrumental music to help you stay focused.

- **Managing Digital Distractions:**
    - **Turn off notifications:** One of the biggest culprits of lost focus is constant notifications from your phone, email, or social media. Turn off non-essential notifications during work periods.
    - **Use focus apps:** Tools like "Focus@Will" or "RescueTime" can help you stay on track by blocking distracting websites or tracking how you spend your time online.
    - **Batch tasks:** Instead of checking your email or messages constantly, set designated times throughout the day for communication. This reduces interruptions and allows you to focus on deeper tasks.

## The Power of Positive Habits

Developing habits that support mental clarity and focus requires consistency and intention. Building these habits over time will help you stay mentally sharp and focused even during high-pressure situations.

- **Create Morning and Evening Routines for Clarity:**
    - **Morning routine:** Start your day with habits that set a positive tone for focus, such as mindfulness exercises, stretching, and reviewing your goals for the day. A structured morning routine helps prepare your mind for the tasks ahead.
    - **Evening routine:** Just as important as starting your day right is ending it well. Wind down by reflecting on your accomplishments, journaling, and setting intentions for the next day. This process helps clear your mind for restful sleep and prepares you for success tomorrow.
- **Building Mental Discipline:**
    - **Stay committed:** Focus and clarity are built through practice. Commit to regular meditation, focused work sessions, and distraction-free periods. The more you practice, the easier it becomes to maintain focus.
    - **Tracking progress:** Keep track of how well you're doing in maintaining focus. Journaling about your distractions and wins can help you identify patterns and refine your routine.

## Nutrition and Hydration for Mental Clarity

What you eat and drink throughout the day has a direct impact on your brain's ability to stay focused. Consuming nutrient-dense foods and staying hydrated can significantly enhance mental performance and clarity.

- **Brain-Boosting Foods:**
    - **Omega-3 fatty acids:** Found in foods like salmon, walnuts, and flaxseeds, omega-3s are essential for brain health and cognitive function.

- **Antioxidants:** Berries, leafy greens, and dark chocolate are rich in antioxidants, which protect the brain from oxidative stress and improve memory and focus.
- **Complex carbohydrates:** Foods like whole grains, legumes, and vegetables provide steady energy to keep your brain sharp throughout the day.

- **Hydration for Focus:**
    - **Stay hydrated:** Dehydration can lead to brain fog and decreased concentration. Keep a water bottle nearby and aim to drink throughout the day.
    - **Limit caffeine:** While caffeine can boost alertness, too much of it can lead to energy crashes and anxiety. Balance your intake with water and herbal teas for sustained energy.

# Chapter 5: Routines for Personal Growth and Learning

Personal growth and learning are essential components of a fulfilling and successful life. Continuous learning not only helps you stay relevant in an ever-changing world but also enriches your mind, fuels your creativity, and pushes you toward becoming the best version of yourself. However, with busy schedules and endless distractions, it can be difficult to prioritize personal development.

Establishing routines that focus on learning and self-improvement allows you to grow consistently, one step at a time. In this chapter, we'll explore practical ways to incorporate personal growth into your daily routine, making it a natural and rewarding part of your life.

## Making Time for Learning

Incorporating learning into your routine doesn't mean you have to dedicate hours to studying or reading each day. By making small but consistent efforts, you can expand your knowledge and skills without overwhelming your schedule.

- **The Power of Small, Consistent Efforts:**
    - **Micro-learning:** Instead of committing to long study sessions, break your learning into smaller, manageable chunks. Spend 15-30 minutes a day learning something

new. Over time, these small efforts compound into significant growth.

- ○ **Leverage downtime:** Use short periods of free time to learn. Whether it's during your commute, while waiting for an appointment, or while exercising, you can listen to podcasts, audiobooks, or educational videos.

- ○ **Set learning goals:** At the beginning of each week or month, set specific goals for what you want to learn. For example, decide to finish a book, complete an online course, or improve a particular skill by the end of the month. Breaking your learning into goals provides direction and motivation.

- **Daily Learning Habits:**

    - ○ **Reading:** Set aside 20-30 minutes each day to read, whether it's a book, article, or research paper. Reading not only expands your knowledge but also stimulates critical thinking and creativity.

    - ○ **Podcasts and audiobooks:** If you're short on time, podcasts and audiobooks offer a convenient way to learn while multitasking. Listen to educational content during your commute, workout, or while doing household chores.

# Embracing a Growth Mindset

A growth mindset is the belief that your abilities and intelligence can be developed through dedication and hard work. This mindset fosters a love for learning and resilience in the face of challenges.

- **What is a Growth Mindset?**

    - ○ **Fixed mindset vs. growth mindset:** People with a fixed mindset believe their talents and intelligence are static, while those with a growth mindset believe they can improve through effort and learning. Adopting a growth mindset encourages you to see challenges as opportunities for improvement rather than roadblocks.

- o **Embrace failure:** Failure is an inevitable part of growth. Instead of seeing it as a setback, view it as feedback for improvement. Analyze what went wrong, learn from it, and apply those lessons to future efforts.

- **Cultivating a Growth Mindset in Your Routine:**

    - o **Practice self-reflection:** Regularly reflect on your progress and the areas you want to improve. Ask yourself, "What did I learn today?" or "How can I do better next time?" Reflection promotes self-awareness and continuous improvement.

    - o **Celebrate progress, not just results:** Focus on the small wins along your learning journey. Recognize and celebrate the effort you're putting into your growth, even if the final results haven't manifested yet. This keeps you motivated to continue learning.

# Scheduling Time for Skill Development

Beyond consuming information, personal growth requires actively applying what you've learned. Building new skills takes practice, and creating dedicated time for skill development is key to ensuring progress.

- **Skill Development Routines:**

    - o **Practice deliberately:** Instead of passively engaging with new information, actively apply what you've learned through deliberate practice. Whether it's improving your writing, coding, or communication skills, focus on consistent and intentional practice.

- **Create project-based goals:** One of the most effective ways to develop new skills is by setting project-based goals. For example, if you're learning photography, set a goal to create a photo portfolio within a certain timeframe. If you're improving your writing, set a goal to publish a blog post or article each week.

- **Join communities of learners:** Surrounding yourself with others who are committed to personal growth can provide encouragement and accountability. Join communities, both online and offline, where you can share your progress, ask questions, and learn from others' experiences.

- **The Power of Mastery:**
  - **Focus on mastery over perfection:** The goal of skill development should be mastery, not perfection. Mastery involves continually improving your skills over time, while perfection can lead to frustration and stagnation. Embrace the process of getting better with each effort.

# Continuous Learning Through Curiosity

Curiosity is the engine that drives lifelong learning. When you cultivate curiosity, you open yourself up to new experiences, ideas, and perspectives. Fostering a sense of wonder and exploration in your daily routine keeps your mind sharp and engaged.

- **Curiosity as a Daily Practice:**
  - **Ask more questions:** Whether you're in a meeting, reading a book, or observing your surroundings, get

into the habit of asking questions. Asking "Why?" or "How?" sparks curiosity and encourages deeper understanding.

- **Explore new topics:** Step outside your comfort zone and explore topics you're unfamiliar with. Whether it's learning about a different culture, field of study, or hobby, expanding your horizons keeps your mind open to new ideas.

- **Embrace learning from others:** Engage in conversations with people who have different viewpoints or experiences. Learning from others not only broadens your knowledge but also helps you see the world through different lenses.

## Developing a Reading Routine

Reading is one of the most powerful tools for personal growth and learning. Whether you're exploring fiction, nonfiction, or educational material, reading enhances your cognitive abilities, stimulates creativity, and provides you with new insights.

- **How to Build a Reading Habit:**
    - **Set reading goals:** Decide how many books you want to read each month or year. Breaking it down into daily or weekly reading sessions makes the goal more manageable. For instance, aim to read 10-20 pages a day or 30 minutes before bed.

    - **Choose a mix of topics:** Reading a variety of genres and subjects—such as biographies, self-improvement, history, or science fiction—exposes you to different perspectives and expands your intellectual horizons.

- **Track your progress:** Keep a reading log or use apps like Goodreads to track the books you've read and the ones you want to read. Tracking progress provides motivation and helps you stay committed to your reading goals.

## Journaling for Self-Reflection and Growth

Journaling is an effective way to organize your thoughts, reflect on your progress, and gain clarity on your personal growth journey. Writing down your experiences, goals, and lessons learned helps solidify what you've absorbed and provides a space for introspection.

- **Daily Journaling Routine:**
    - **Reflect on your day:** At the end of each day, spend 10-15 minutes reflecting on what you've learned, what went well, and what challenges you faced. Journaling your thoughts helps you process your experiences and identify areas for growth.
    - **Goal setting through journaling:** Use your journal to set and track personal growth goals. Write down specific, actionable steps you plan to take, and periodically review your progress to ensure you stay on track.
    - **Gratitude and learning:** Combine gratitude with journaling by reflecting on what you're thankful for and what you've learned. Gratitude shifts your mindset toward positivity and encourages a growth-oriented perspective.

# Chapter 6: Evening Routines for Reflection and Relaxation

While much attention is often given to morning routines, how you end your day can be just as important. An intentional evening routine allows you to wind down, reflect on the day's events, and prepare for restful sleep. These moments of calm and reflection not only help you recover from the day's challenges but also lay the groundwork for a productive tomorrow.

In this chapter, we will explore the essential components of a well-rounded evening routine that fosters relaxation, reflection, and readiness for the day ahead. By embracing these practices, you'll build a framework for better mental, emotional, and physical well-being.

## The Importance of an Evening Routine

Why is an evening routine so crucial? The way you transition from the busyness of the day into rest can determine how well you sleep and how you feel the next morning. Without structure, your mind may stay overstimulated, leading to restless sleep and a lack of focus the following day. A thoughtful evening routine helps you establish closure, restore your energy, and prepare both mentally and physically for another productive day.

- **Mental Unwinding:**

- o **Mental closure:** After a busy day, it's important to let go of unresolved thoughts or worries. An evening routine creates a mental "closing bell" for the day, signaling your brain to transition into rest mode.

- o **Reduced decision fatigue:** Making decisions throughout the day can drain your mental energy. An evening routine helps you eliminate unnecessary decisions (such as deciding what to wear or eat tomorrow) and prepares you for a smooth start in the morning.

- **Physical Relaxation:**

  - o **Activating the parasympathetic nervous system:** An evening routine that includes relaxation techniques like deep breathing or gentle stretching activates your parasympathetic nervous system, which is responsible for rest and recovery. This helps lower stress levels and signals to your body that it's time to wind down.

  - o **Prepping your body for sleep:** Your body needs cues that it's time to slow down and prepare for sleep. By dimming the lights, limiting screen time, and engaging in calming activities, you can improve your sleep quality and overall well-being.

## Crafting a Calming Evening Environment

The environment in which you spend your evenings plays a significant role in how easily you can relax. A cluttered or overstimulating environment can make it difficult to transition from work mode to rest mode. On the other hand, a serene and comfortable setting helps your mind and body let go of the day's stress.

- **Decluttering for Peace of Mind:**

- o **Evening declutter session:** Spend 5-10 minutes tidying up your living and sleeping space. Clear away distractions like clutter, papers, or laundry that can create a sense of chaos. This simple act helps create a feeling of calm and control.

- o **Minimalism for mental clarity:** The less visual clutter in your space, the easier it is for your mind to relax. Focus on creating an environment with minimal distractions—a clean and simple space can help clear mental clutter as well.

- **Lighting for Relaxation:**

  - o **Dim the lights:** Bright artificial light signals to your brain that it's still daytime, making it harder to produce melatonin, the hormone that regulates sleep. Dimming your lights or using soft, warm lighting in the evening encourages the body's natural sleep rhythm.

  - o **Use natural light cues:** If possible, align your evening routine with natural light. As the sun sets, your body is naturally programmed to wind down. You can enhance this by using candles or lamps with soft light rather than harsh overhead lighting.

- **Comfort as a Sleep Aid:**

  - o **Invest in comfort:** Your bedroom should be your sanctuary for rest. Invest in comfortable bedding, pillows, and blankets that make you look forward to sleep. Consider upgrading your mattress or adding extra layers for maximum comfort.

  - o **Sleep temperature:** Keep your bedroom cool. Studies show that the optimal temperature for sleep is between 60-67°F (15-20°C). Cooler environments promote deeper sleep, helping your body regulate its temperature during the night.

# Evening Reflection: Looking Back at Your Day

Reflection is a critical aspect of personal growth. Taking time to evaluate your day allows you to process emotions, learn from experiences, and let go of any lingering stress. Reflecting in the evening also helps you create closure, so you don't carry unresolved thoughts into the next day.

- **Daily Journaling:**
    - **Structured reflection:** Spend 10-15 minutes each evening journaling about your day. Write down what you accomplished, what challenges you faced, and what you learned. This simple practice helps you gain clarity and recognize patterns in your behavior or thinking.
    - **Questions to ask yourself:** Reflect on the following:
        - What went well today?
        - What didn't go as planned, and how can I improve tomorrow?
        - Did I achieve my goals, or did I encounter unexpected challenges?
        - How did I manage stress or difficult situations?
    - **Learning from your day:** Journaling isn't just about venting frustrations or listing accomplishments—it's about learning from your experiences. This reflective practice helps you see how you can improve, making each day a step toward personal growth.
- **Gratitude Practice for Positive Reflection:**
    - **Why gratitude matters:** Practicing gratitude shifts your focus from stress or negativity to the positive aspects of your life. It promotes a mindset of abundance

and contentment, which can improve your overall well-being and sleep quality.

- **Daily gratitude exercise:** At the end of each day, write down three things you're grateful for. These can be small moments (like a conversation with a friend) or larger achievements (like completing a project). Gratitude helps you focus on the positive, reducing stress and promoting restful sleep.
- **Shifting your mindset:** Gratitude not only improves sleep but also enhances your overall outlook on life. When you consistently reflect on what you appreciate, you train your brain to focus more on the positives in everyday life.

## Preparing for Tomorrow: Setting Yourself Up for Success

The evening is the perfect time to organize and plan for the day ahead. By doing so, you reduce the stress of having to rush through decisions in the morning and ensure that you wake up feeling prepared and focused.

- **Set Priorities for Tomorrow:**
    - **Review tomorrow's schedule:** Take 5-10 minutes to look over your calendar and to-do list for the next day. This helps you mentally prepare for what's coming and avoid surprises.
    - **Identify your MITs:** Your Most Important Tasks (MITs) are the top 2-3 things that must get done tomorrow. By identifying these in the evening, you reduce decision fatigue and ensure that you're focusing on what truly matters when you wake up.

- - **Batch smaller tasks:** If you have smaller tasks that can be grouped together (like checking emails or running errands), schedule time for them in your day. Batching similar tasks saves mental energy and increases efficiency.

- **Prepare Materials and Essentials:**
  - **Lay out your clothes:** Save time in the morning by deciding on your outfit the night before. Whether it's work attire or casual wear, having your clothes ready reduces the number of decisions you need to make in the morning.
  - **Organize your work materials:** If you have meetings, projects, or work tasks scheduled for the next day, organize everything you need before bed. This might include packing your bag, charging your devices, or laying out necessary paperwork. Being prepared eliminates stress and ensures a smoother start to the day.

- **Visualize Tomorrow's Success:**
  - **Positive visualization:** Before bed, take a few moments to visualize a successful tomorrow. Picture yourself completing your tasks, navigating challenges with ease, and feeling accomplished at the end of the day. Visualization strengthens your confidence and prepares your mind for success.
  - **Mental rehearsal:** If you have a specific challenge coming up (such as a meeting or presentation), mentally rehearse how you will approach it. This helps reduce anxiety and boosts performance by creating a sense of readiness.

# Relaxation Techniques for Better Sleep

Physical relaxation plays a crucial role in preparing your body for sleep. Incorporating relaxation techniques into your evening routine helps reduce stress and signals to your nervous system that it's time to rest.

- **Deep Breathing for Relaxation:**
    - **Breathing exercises:** Focused breathing calms the nervous system and helps relieve tension. One effective technique is box breathing: inhale for 4 seconds, hold for 4 seconds, exhale for 4 seconds, and hold again for 4 seconds. Repeat for 5-10 minutes to promote relaxation.
    - **Diaphragmatic breathing:** Also known as belly breathing, this technique involves breathing deeply into your diaphragm rather than shallowly into your chest. Diaphragmatic breathing reduces stress hormones and encourages full-body relaxation.
- **Progressive Muscle Relaxation:**
    - **How it works:** Progressive muscle relaxation (PMR) involves tensing and then relaxing different muscle groups in your body, one by one. Starting with your feet and working your way up to your head, you focus on each muscle group, tensing it for 5-10 seconds and then releasing.
    - **Benefits:** PMR helps reduce physical tension, making it easier to drift into sleep. It's especially effective if you find yourself carrying stress in certain areas of your body, such as your shoulders or neck.
- **Gentle Evening Yoga:**

- **Yoga for relaxation:** Gentle yoga or stretching before bed can help release physical tension and prepare your body for sleep. Poses like forward bends, child's pose, and seated twists promote relaxation and calm the mind.

- **Bedtime yoga routine:** A short bedtime yoga routine (5-15 minutes) can help stretch out tight muscles, ease back pain, and calm your nervous system. Focus on slow, mindful movements and deep breathing to encourage relaxation.

## Establishing a Consistent Sleep Schedule

Consistency is one of the most important factors in maintaining good sleep hygiene. By going to bed and waking up at the same time each day, you help regulate your body's circadian rhythm, making it easier to fall asleep and wake up feeling refreshed.

- **Sticking to a Schedule:**
    - **Set a consistent bedtime:** Try to go to bed and wake up at the same time every day, even on weekends. This consistency trains your body to follow a natural sleep-wake cycle, improving your sleep quality over time.
    - **Wind down naturally:** Start winding down at least 30-60 minutes before your scheduled bedtime. Use this time to engage in calming activities like reading, journaling, or practicing relaxation techniques.
- **Avoiding Sleep Disruptors:**
    - **Limit stimulants:** Avoid caffeine, nicotine, or heavy meals at least 4-6 hours before bedtime. These stimulants can interfere with your ability to fall asleep and disrupt your sleep cycle.

- **Create a screen-free zone:** blue light from phones, tablets, and computers can delay the release of melatonin, making it harder to fall asleep. Make your bedroom a screen-free zone at least 30-60 minutes before bed to promote better sleep.

Your evening routine is a powerful tool for relaxation, reflection, and preparation for the day ahead. By intentionally crafting a routine that helps you unwind, reflect on your day, and prepare for tomorrow, you set the stage for deeper sleep and a more productive tomorrow. With consistency, these habits will help you end each day on a positive note and wake up feeling refreshed, focused, and ready to tackle whatever challenges come your way.

# Chapter 7: Routines to Build Strong Relationships

While productivity and personal growth are essential to success, strong relationships are equally important. The connections you build with others—whether family, friends, colleagues, or partners—form the foundation for support, collaboration, and emotional well-being. However, just like any other aspect of life, relationships require intentional effort to thrive.

Establishing routines that prioritize communication, empathy, and quality time can help you nurture these relationships and foster deeper connections. In this chapter, we will explore how to build and sustain meaningful relationships by incorporating relationship-strengthening habits into your daily and weekly routines.

## The Importance of Building Strong Relationships

Strong relationships are essential not only for emotional well-being but also for success in both personal and professional life. Meaningful connections with others provide support during challenging times, enhance your happiness, and contribute to personal growth.

- **Emotional Support:**
    - **Why emotional connection matters:** Having people you can turn to for support, encouragement, or simply to share experiences with is crucial for maintaining

balance. These connections help reduce stress, provide perspective, and reinforce your sense of belonging.

- **Shared successes and challenges:** Celebrating your successes with others amplifies your joy, while sharing your challenges creates a sense of solidarity. Knowing that someone cares about your journey can be a source of motivation and emotional resilience.

- **The Social Aspect of Success:**

    - **Collaborative success:** Strong relationships often lead to opportunities for collaboration. In professional settings, fostering good relationships can open doors to partnerships, mentorships, and new ventures. In personal life, your relationships help create a support network that enables you to pursue your goals.

    - **Loneliness vs. connection:** In a world where digital communication is the norm, it's easy to feel disconnected even when you're constantly "in touch." Building meaningful, in-person connections combats loneliness and adds depth to your interactions.

## Communication as the Foundation of Strong Relationships

Communication is the bedrock of any relationship. Whether it's a quick check-in with a friend or a deep conversation with a partner, regular communication fosters trust, understanding, and emotional intimacy. Incorporating intentional communication into your daily routine ensures that your relationships stay strong, even in the busiest times.

- **Daily and Weekly Communication Routines:**

- **Check-in with loved ones:** Make it a habit to check in with the important people in your life regularly. Whether it's a daily text, a phone call, or a face-to-face conversation, these small touchpoints show that you care and are thinking of them.
- **Weekly catch-ups:** For friends or family members you don't see daily, set aside time each week for a phone call, coffee, or video chat. These longer catch-ups help maintain deeper relationships and create space for more meaningful conversations.

- **Active Listening:**
    - **What is active listening?** Active listening means fully focusing on the speaker, understanding their message, and responding thoughtfully. This builds trust and shows that you value what the other person has to say.
    - **How to practice active listening:** When someone is speaking, avoid interrupting or thinking ahead to your response. Instead, make eye contact, nod in acknowledgment, and ask follow-up questions to clarify their thoughts. Summarizing or paraphrasing their points shows that you've been paying attention.

- **Clear and Honest Communication:**
    - **Expressing needs and feelings:** Being open and honest about your needs, emotions, and boundaries is key to maintaining healthy relationships. It prevents misunderstandings and resentment from building up over time.
    - **Approaching difficult conversations:** Approach challenging topics with empathy and a willingness to listen. Focus on understanding the other person's perspective rather than jumping to defend your own.

# Quality Time as a Relationship-Strengthening Routine

Spending quality time with the important people in your life is essential for building and sustaining strong relationships. In today's busy world, it's easy to take loved ones for granted or let time together become routine and impersonal. Creating regular opportunities for meaningful interactions can help deepen your connections and ensure that your relationships continue to grow.

- **Prioritizing Quality Over Quantity:**
    - **Intentional time together:** The key to quality time is not just spending time together but being fully present during that time. Whether it's having dinner with family, going on a walk with a friend, or simply talking, focus on being engaged and attentive.
    - **Eliminate distractions:** Make an effort to disconnect from technology and other distractions when you're spending time with loved ones. Putting your phone away during conversations shows that you value the person's presence and are fully focused on them.
- **Creating Rituals for Connection:**
    - **Weekly or monthly traditions:** Establish regular rituals that allow you to reconnect with the important people in your life. This could be a weekly family dinner, a monthly game night with friends, or a quarterly catch-up with a mentor. These rituals give you something to look forward to and provide a consistent opportunity for connection.
    - **Celebrate milestones and successes:** Make a habit of celebrating milestones—whether big or small—with the people who matter most. This could be anything from promotions, birthdays, or personal achievements. Taking the time to acknowledge and celebrate successes strengthens your bond.

- **Incorporating Spontaneity:**
    - **Surprise gestures:** Every now and then, surprise your loved ones with spontaneous acts of kindness. This could be as simple as leaving a note for your partner, bringing coffee to a colleague, or planning a surprise visit for a friend. These small gestures go a long way in showing appreciation and keeping the relationship vibrant.
    - **Be open to spontaneity:** While routines are important, being open to last-minute plans or impromptu moments of connection can also strengthen relationships. Saying yes to spontaneous opportunities to connect shows flexibility and excitement to engage with others.

## Building Empathy and Understanding in Relationships

Empathy—the ability to understand and share the feelings of another person—is a cornerstone of healthy relationships. Cultivating empathy through your daily actions and mindset can deepen your connections, improve communication, and help you navigate difficult situations with grace.

- **Practicing Empathy in Everyday Life:**
    - **Putting yourself in their shoes:** Make an effort to consider the other person's perspective before reacting. Ask yourself how they might be feeling and why they might be acting a certain way. This practice helps you respond with more compassion and understanding.
    - **Acknowledge feelings:** When someone expresses their emotions to you, acknowledge their feelings, even if you don't agree with their perspective. Phrases like "I understand why you feel that way" or "It sounds like

that was really difficult for you" show that you're validating their experience.

- **Navigating Conflict with Empathy:**
    - **Stay calm and listen:** During conflicts, it's easy to get caught up in defending your point of view. Instead, pause, listen to the other person's concerns, and acknowledge their emotions. This helps de-escalate tension and fosters a more productive conversation.
    - **Focus on solutions, not blame:** Rather than focusing on who's right or wrong, shift the conversation toward finding a solution that addresses both parties' needs. Empathy in conflict resolution leads to better outcomes and helps preserve the relationship.

## Balancing Relationships and Personal Growth

While nurturing relationships is essential, maintaining a balance between your personal growth and your connections with others is key to long-term success and happiness. Striking this balance allows you to support the people you care about while also honouring your own needs and goals.

- **Setting Healthy Boundaries:**
    - **Communicate your limits:** Healthy boundaries protect both you and your relationships. Be clear about your personal limits—whether it's needing alone time, managing your workload, or addressing emotional needs—and communicate these boundaries openly with those around you.
    - **Respect others' boundaries:** Just as you set boundaries, it's important to respect the boundaries of

others. This shows that you value their well-being and understand their need for personal space or time.

- **Incorporating Personal Development into Relationships:**
    - **Support each other's growth:** A strong relationship doesn't just focus on the connection between two people—it also supports each person's individual growth. Encourage your friends, family, or partner to pursue their goals, and ask for the same support in return.
    - **Pursue shared goals:** If possible, work toward shared goals together. Whether it's learning a new skill, improving fitness, or embarking on a creative project, shared goals help strengthen bonds and provide a sense of accomplishment.

## Building and Maintaining Professional Relationships

Strong relationships in your personal life are important, but professional relationships can also play a significant role in your success. Networking, collaboration, and mentorship are essential components of career development, and establishing routines to build and maintain these relationships can open doors to new opportunities.

- **Networking as a Routine:**
    - **Reach out regularly:** Don't wait until you need something to connect with people in your professional network. Make it a habit to reach out to colleagues, mentors, and industry contacts regularly. Send a quick message to check in, share an article, or catch up over coffee.
    - **Attend networking events:** Schedule time each month to attend networking events, conferences, or industry

meetups. Building relationships in person helps establish trust and opens up opportunities for collaboration.

- **Mentorship and Professional Support:**
    - **Find a mentor:** Mentorship is a powerful tool for personal and professional growth. If you don't have a mentor, consider reaching out to someone you admire in your field. Establish a routine for regular check-ins or discussions to learn from their experiences.
    - **Be a mentor:** Just as it's important to receive guidance, offering mentorship to others can be rewarding and mutually beneficial. By supporting the growth of others, you not only strengthen your professional relationships but also gain fresh perspectives.

Strong relationships don't just happen—they require effort, communication, and intentional routines. Whether it's staying connected with loved ones, practicing empathy, or investing time in professional networks, building strong relationships is a key ingredient for long-term success and happiness. By incorporating these routines into your daily and weekly life, you'll create a solid foundation of trust, support, and connection that enhances every aspect of your personal and professional journey.

# Chapter 8: Customizing and Evolving Your Routines

Routines are essential tools for creating structure, building habits, and achieving success. However, life is dynamic, and as your goals, priorities, and circumstances change, so too must your routines. A routine that serves you well today may need adjustments as you grow and evolve. Customizing and evolving your routines ensures that they continue to support your development and help you reach new heights.

In this chapter, we'll explore how to tailor your routines to suit your unique needs and how to adjust them as your life and goals evolve. By maintaining flexibility and openness to change, you can create a routine that grows with you, rather than one that limits you.

## Understanding the Purpose of Your Routines

Before making changes to your routines, it's important to understand the "why" behind them. Your routines should align with your goals and values, supporting both your personal and professional growth. Reflecting on the purpose of your routines will help you decide which aspects are working and which need adjustment.

- **Aligning Routines with Goals:**
    - **Reflect on your current routines:** Take time to analyze your existing routines. Ask yourself, "Why did I start this routine?" and "Is it still serving its original

purpose?" If your goals have shifted, your routine may need to adapt as well.

- o **Evaluate the impact:** Consider how your routines are contributing to or detracting from your goals. If a routine no longer serves a positive purpose or feels like an obligation without benefits, it may be time to let it go or modify it.

- **Connecting Routines to Core Values:**

    - o **Identify your core values:** Your routines should reflect what matters most to you. Whether it's health, personal growth, family, or career success, your routines should align with your values and help you live in accordance with them.

    - o **Purpose-driven routines:** If a routine isn't aligned with your values, it can become a source of frustration. Reflect on how each part of your routine serves your deeper purpose and adjust it to better fit your values.

## Assessing and Adjusting Your Routines

Routines are not set in stone. To ensure that they continue to serve you, it's essential to periodically assess and adjust them based on your current needs, goals, and circumstances. By doing this, you keep your routines fresh, relevant, and aligned with your growth.

- **Regular Routine Check-ins:**

    - o **Set a routine review schedule:** Every few months, schedule time to review your routines. This could be quarterly or at the end of each season. During these check-ins, evaluate what's working, what's not, and what adjustments are necessary.

    - o **Ask key questions:** Reflect on questions such as:

- Are my routines helping me move closer to my goals?
- Do I feel energized and motivated by my routines, or are they draining?
- Have my circumstances changed, requiring adjustments to my routine?
- What new habits do I want to incorporate, and which habits can I let go of?

- **Making Incremental Changes:**
    - **Tweak small aspects:** Instead of overhauling your entire routine, focus on making small, incremental changes. For example, if your morning routine feels rushed, add just 10 extra minutes for a calming activity, like stretching or meditation.
    - **Adjust to new priorities:** As your life evolves, so will your priorities. If you've recently taken on a new role at work or started a personal project, adjust your routine to reflect these new priorities. This might mean reducing time spent on less important tasks and reallocating it to higher-priority activities.

# Creating Flexibility Within Your Routine

One of the biggest challenges with routines is that they can become too rigid, leaving little room for spontaneity, creativity, or unexpected events. Flexibility within your routine allows you to adapt to life's inevitable changes while maintaining consistency in the habits that matter most.

- **Structured Flexibility:**

- **Plan for flexibility:** Include flexibility as part of your routine. For example, block off time in your schedule for "buffer periods" where you can handle unexpected tasks or enjoy spontaneous activities. These buffer periods prevent your routine from feeling overly restrictive.
- **Avoid perfectionism:** It's important to recognize that not every day will go exactly as planned. Be kind to yourself if you deviate from your routine occasionally. The goal is consistency over time, not perfection every single day.

- **Adapting to Changes:**
  - **Seasonal adjustments:** Your routine may need to change with the seasons. For example, during the summer, you may have more outdoor activities, while in the winter, you may need to focus more on indoor routines. Allow your routine to shift naturally with the seasons, reflecting the ebb and flow of your life.
  - **Embrace change:** Life is full of unexpected events, from travel to personal milestones. Instead of clinging to a routine during these times, embrace the changes and adapt your routine accordingly. For instance, when traveling, modify your exercise or work routine to fit the new environment.

## Experimenting with New Habits

Just as old routines may need to be adjusted, new habits can be introduced to reflect your current aspirations. Experimenting with new habits allows you to discover what works best for you and keeps your routine fresh and engaging.

- **The Power of Habit Stacking:**

- What is habit stacking? Habit stacking involves adding a new habit to an existing one, making it easier to incorporate the new habit into your routine. For example, if you already have a morning coffee ritual, you can stack a new habit, like reading for 10 minutes, right after your coffee.

- How to implement habit stacking: Identify habits you already perform regularly, such as brushing your teeth, having lunch, or checking your email. Stack new habits onto these existing ones, creating a natural flow between activities.

- **Embrace Trial and Error:**
  - **Test new habits:** Not every new habit will work for you, and that's okay. Allow yourself to experiment with different routines or practices to see what feels best. For instance, you might try journaling in the morning for a week, and if it doesn't feel right, you can try it in the evening instead.

  - **Reflect on outcomes:** After a period of experimenting with new habits, reflect on how they make you feel. Do they enhance your focus, reduce stress, or help you achieve your goals? If a new habit feels beneficial, integrate it more permanently into your routine.

## Letting Go of Routines That No Longer Serve You

Just as it's important to introduce new habits, it's equally important to recognize when a routine no longer serves your best interests. Holding onto old routines out of habit or obligation can hinder your growth. Letting go of these routines creates space for new opportunities and more fulfilling habits.

- **Recognizing When to Let Go:**

- o **Signs of a stale routine:** If a routine feels like a chore, leaves you feeling drained, or no longer aligns with your goals, it may be time to let it go. Consider whether the routine is serving your current needs or whether it's simply a holdover from a past version of yourself.
- o **Embrace change:** Change can be uncomfortable, but it's essential for growth. By letting go of routines that no longer serve you, you make room for new opportunities, experiences, and personal development.

- **Guilt-Free Adjustment:**
  - o **Release the guilt:** It's common to feel guilty about changing or abandoning routines, especially if you've invested a lot of time in them. However, it's important to recognize that your routine is there to serve you, not the other way around. Letting go of an outdated routine is a sign of growth, not failure.
  - o **Focus on progress:** Instead of feeling guilty about what you're leaving behind, focus on the new routines and habits you're cultivating. Celebrate the progress you're making and the ways your routine is evolving to support your current needs.

## Adapting Your Routine to Different Life Phases

Throughout your life, you will go through different phases, each with its own demands and challenges. As your life changes—whether due to career shifts, personal relationships, or major life events—your routines should adapt to reflect these transitions.

- **Adapting to Career and Life Changes:**
  - o **Career transitions:** If you're starting a new job, launching a business, or transitioning to a different

career, your routine will need to shift to accommodate new responsibilities and goals. Adjust your work routine to reflect your new priorities, while still maintaining a balance with personal habits.

- o **Major life events:** Big life changes, such as moving to a new city, getting married, or becoming a parent, will naturally affect your routines. Be flexible and open to adjusting your habits to fit your new reality, while holding onto the core routines that support your well-being.

- **Routines for Different Stages of Life:**

    - o **Young adulthood:** In early adulthood, your routines may focus on building a career, developing new skills, and exploring personal interests. Flexibility and experimentation are key during this phase, as you're discovering what works best for you.

    - o **Midlife:** As you reach midlife, your routines may become more focused on balancing career success with family and personal fulfillment. This is a time to reassess your priorities and ensure that your routines reflect your evolving goals.

    - o **Later life:** In later life, routines may shift toward maintaining health, enjoying leisure activities, and staying connected with loved ones. The focus may shift from achievement-driven routines to those that promote well-being, connection, and personal satisfaction.

# Conclusion

As you've seen throughout this book, success is not achieved overnight—it's built through consistent, intentional actions taken day after day. Your routines are the foundation on which you create a life of productivity, growth, and fulfillment. They provide the structure you need to focus on your goals, maintain balance, and overcome challenges, all while allowing space for reflection and relaxation.

By implementing the routines we've explored, you now have the tools to:

- Start your mornings with purpose and energy.
- Build a productive work routine that maximizes focus.
- Integrate healthy habits into your daily life for sustained physical and mental well-being.
- Cultivate mental clarity and adaptability in a fast-paced world.
- Prioritize personal growth and continuous learning.
- Strengthen relationships with loved ones and colleagues.
- Reflect and unwind in the evenings to ensure each day is a step forward.

But remember, routines are meant to evolve. As your goals and circumstances change, your routines will need to adapt. Stay flexible, regularly reassess your habits, and be open to experimenting with new strategies. The key is to ensure that your routines continue to align with your values and support your growth.

Success is not just about reaching a destination—it's about the journey you take every single day. By mastering your routines, you are creating a system that empowers you to live with purpose, achieve your goals, and enjoy a more balanced, fulfilling life.

Thank you for taking this journey toward success with me. Now, it's time to take action and make your routines work for you. Keep evolving, keep growing, and remember that each day is an opportunity to move closer to the life you desire.

# Take Your Productivity to the Next Level!

Thank you for reading "ROUTINES FOR SUCCESS." If you're ready to dive even deeper into mastering your time and boosting your productivity, I invite you to check out my first book in the MASTERY IN PRODUCTIVITY series: **"Master Your Time: A Comprehensive guide to productivity and balance"**

In "MASTER YOUR TIME," you'll discover:

- Time management techniques that help you reclaim your day.
- Practical tools to eliminate distractions and maximize focus.
- Step-by-step strategies to align your tasks with your biggest goals.

Whether you're looking to supercharge your personal productivity or create a better work-life balance, "MASTER YOUR TIME" provides the insights and actionable advice you need to take full control of your schedule.

Don't let time slip away—take the next step on your journey to success!

# Bibliography

- **Clear, James.** ATOMIC HABITS: AN EASY & PROVEN WAY TO BUILD GOOD HABITS & BREAK BAD ONES. Avery, 2018.

- **Duhigg, Charles.** THE POWER OF HABIT: WHY WE DO WHAT WE DO IN LIFE AND BUSINESS. Random House, 2012.

- **Hyatt, Michael.** FREE TO FOCUS: A TOTAL PRODUCTIVITY SYSTEM TO ACHIEVE MORE BY DOING LESS. Baker Books, 2019.

- **Keller, Gary, and Jay Papasan.** THE ONE THING: THE SURPRISINGLY SIMPLE TRUTH BEHIND EXTRAORDINARY RESULTS. Bard Press, 2013.

- **Robinson, Ken, and Lou Aronica.** FINDING YOUR ELEMENT: HOW TO DISCOVER YOUR TALENTS AND PASSIONS AND TRANSFORM YOUR LIFE. Penguin Books, 2013.

- **Roth, Charles H.** WORK SMARTER: LIVE BETTER – PRACTICAL TIME MANAGEMENT STRATEGIES TO GET MORE DONE. Success Factory, 2016.

www.ingramcontent.com/pod-product-compliance
Lightning Source LLC
Chambersburg PA
CBHW030048230526
45471CB00003B/987